HEROES OF THE MOVIES

HEROES OF THE MOVIES

Liza MINNELLI

A biography by Susan D'Arcy

THE CONFUCIAN PRESS, INC.

Heroes of the Movies – Liza Minnelli

Reprinted by arrangement with LSP Books, Ltd., England

ISBN 0-88373-076-1

The Confucian Press, Inc.
8-10 West 36 Street
New York, New York 10018

'Hollywood was my back garden,
my everyday life.
Broadway was different and exciting'
—Liza Minnelli

"She was, of course, the most beautiful baby in the nursery. There alone on a table, was a perfect child, with absolutely no wrinkles," wrote an understandably biased Vincente Minnelli about his infant daughter, Liza. A friend told him sympathetically "Don't worry, she'll grow into those eyes … "

At the time Liza May Minnelli was born at the Cedars of Lebanon Hospital, Los Angeles on March 12, 1946 many people could have speculated with some assurance that the child of Judy Garland and Vincente Minnelli inherited talent almost as a birthright. But few could have guessed the measure of that talent.

She was a loved child, a cherished child, but her parents were busy people: her mother was one of MGM's biggest dollar earners, her father a brilliant and creative director. Soon after her birth her parents were at work on *The Pirate* and Liza was given over to the capable secure administrations of her nanny, Miss MacFarlane.

As a toddler, Liza had a walk-on appearance in her mother's film *In the Good Old Summertime*, directed by Robert Z Leonard. In 1954 she made a brief appearance in *The Long, Long Trailer*, directed by her father and starring Lucille Ball and Desi Arnaz, but the wedding party sequence in which she appeared ended on the cutting room floor. There was no parental pressure for Liza to become a professional child performer and in this way she probably avoided at least some of the tensions and potential tragedies which were Judy Garland's lot.

Though she spent her childhood on the sets of her parents' films, it wasn't Hollywood that established Liza's bent toward greasepaint. "I was a child of Hollywood, and loved it all, but it was when my parents took me to a Broadway show when I was thirteen that I knew what I wanted to do. From that moment no other life entered my thinking. I fell in love with the theatre. It was magical. I suppose because Hollywood was my back garden, my everyday life, but Broadway was different and exciting."

She remembers as a child being dressed in perfect miniatures of her mother's screen costumes, especially created by Edith Head for diminutive Liza. With her childhood friend, Mia Farrow, she would dance on the lawn in the futile hope that the tour buses would stop and ask who they were.

"The tour buses never stopped," says Liza. "In fact, I'm not even sure they followed that route, but we danced anyway. Then one marvellous day a car drew up. We got terribly excited – fame at last – and we rushed over to the car. There was a man driving and a lady sitting in the back. When we got to the car, the back door opened and the lady leaned out and threw up. That was the reason they stopped – not because they were enchanted with our dancing but because the lady wanted to be sick. We didn't dance on the lawn much after that.

The early security was soon replaced by the uncertainty of being Judy Garland's daughter. The heights and depths of Judy's life had a profound effect on her children but Liza , being older, was more aware of it than either Lorna or Joey Luft. "Being Judy Garland's daughter is only a problem if you start listening to what people are saying," Liza said later, playing down the disadvantages. In 1952 her parents were divorced.

"I guess I must have been affected by it. But it wasn't after all, as though they were going to live on different planets. I always saw an awful lot of my father. He was, and still is, the best friend I've got."

Liza went to school – and hated it – all over the place. "We moved around a lot from house to house, normally in the night. That was probably because Mama was so broke and maybe she owed money to

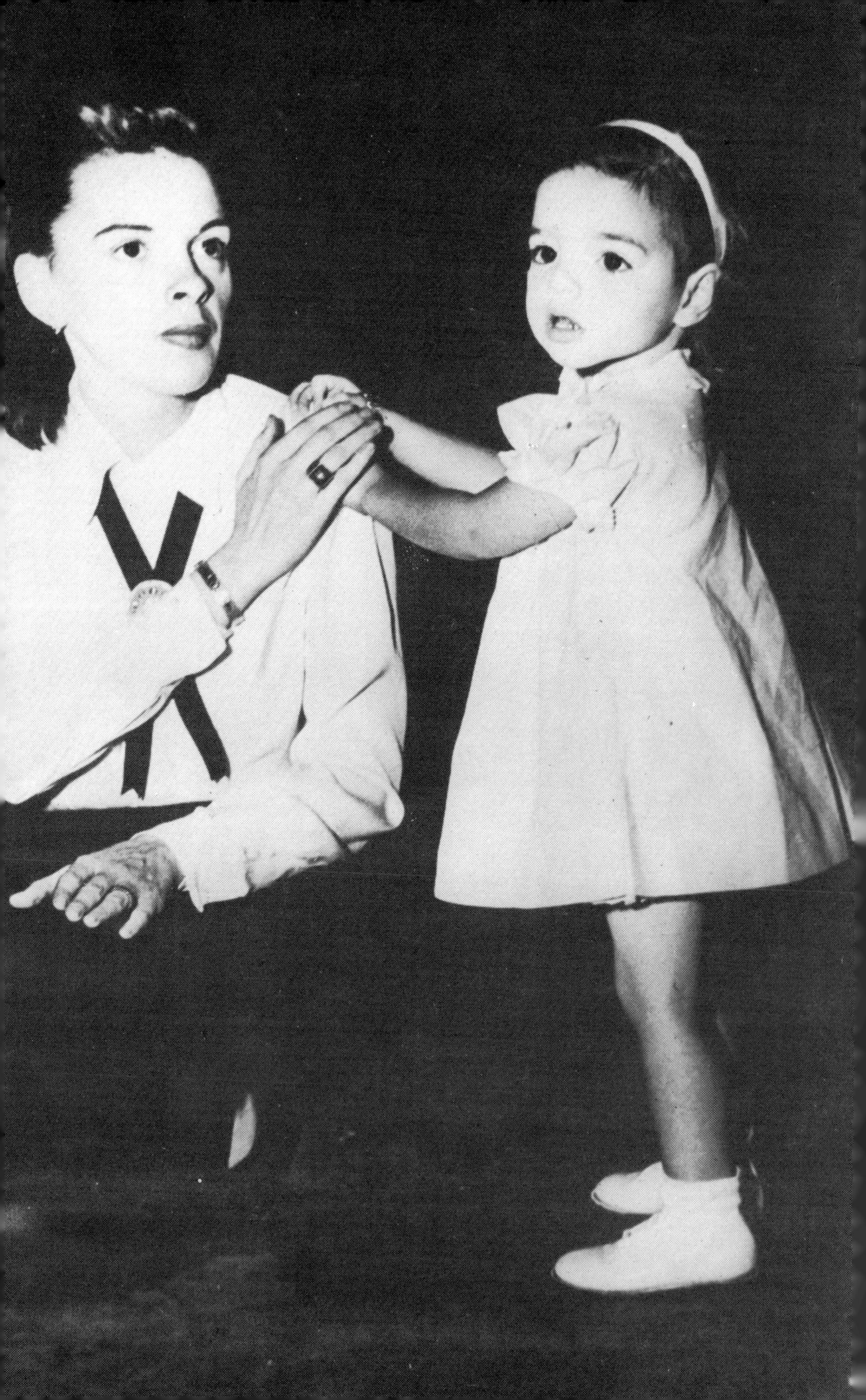

the landlords. Anyway, every time we moved I'd find myself in a different school. Private if we could afford it, public if we couldn't. I hated school, it annoyed me."

The story goes that by the time she was eleven, Liza personally did the hiring and firing of household staff. And at thirteen she was driving Lorna to school because the chaffeur was drunk.

When she was seven, Liza appeared on stage with Judy Garland at the Palace Theatre, New York and danced while Judy sang "Swanee". "I remember hearing waves and waves of applause washing over us. I also remember wondering whether my pants showed." At fourteen Liza starred in a high school production of "The Diary of Anne Frank" which toured Israel, Greece and Italy.

As an adolescent, Liza Minnelli had faced more than her share of catastrophies. Later she would admit quietly, "I was raised with so much drama. I don't crave it. I'm an observer and like to draw a line between what is fantasy and what is not." First hand she saw the alarming rise and fall of Judy Garland's career, but in spite of the traumas and the suicide attempts the good times outweighed the bad. Judy lavished affection and love on the children and looking back Liza remembers the laughter.

When she was sixteen, Liza left home. "Mama went on a kick every now and then and she'd kick me out of the house. Usually I'd stand on the doorstep and we'd fall into each other's arms after a while. One day I took her up on it and went to New York. My father gave me one hundred dollars – the last money I took. I never felt lonely even during the first New York days because I thought I was Ruby Keeler. I just sailed above it all."

In New York Liza showed her determination to succeed not as Judy Garland's daughter but as herself. Auditioning under an assumed name for the fourth lead in "Best Foot Forward" she won the role. "I was testing myself," she says.

Not wanting to steal Liza's limelight on the opening night, Judy Garland attended the second night's performance. "She made a big thing about somebody telling her the opening night was the next night but I knew the real reason she didn't come was because she didn't want to draw the attention away from me."

For her debut in "Best Foot Forward" Liza won the Daniel Blum Award for the year's most promising young actress.

In 1962 Liza was persuaded to provide the voice of Dorothy for the animation feature *Journey Back to Oz*. It was loosely based on L Fred Baum's first sequel to *The Wizard of Oz* and Liza appeared dressed as Dorothy in a montage shot when the cast were introduced at the end. The Monthly Film Bulletin commented: "Liza Minnelli's quiet, intelligent reading of Dorothy strikes just the right note." In America Judy helped promote Liza's efforts, though the feature was not a success and in Britain was not released for another decade.

Together Judy and Liza appeared at the London Palladium in 1964 and it was the first occasion where Liza was receiving her full share of the applause. The puppy fat had gone: Liza Minnelli was a person, not just Judy's daughter. "Mama, at this point, suddenly realised that she had a grown-up daughter: that she wasn't a kid herself any more. I'm sure this happens with almost any mother and daughter but it happened to my mother in front of 8,000 people." It was, Liza recalls, "an orgy of emotion." A friend who was there observed: "Judy was fighting for a love that she had had for a long time. And here was a newcomer taking some of that love."

The following year, 1965, was a good one for Liza. She became the youngest actress ever to win a Tony Award when she starred in "Flora the Red Menace"

off-Broadway. The shows did not do well but Liza got excellent reviews. And because of the show she met Fred Ebb, the song writer who she regards as her Svengali, transforming her from Judy Garland's daughter into Liza Minnelli. He recalls his first meeting with Liza: "She looked awful, like Raggedy Ann. Everything was just a little torn and a little soiled. She just sat there and stared at me, and I stared back." Later he and John Kander would write highly personalised songs for Liza which would give her a new image – "Liza with a Z", "Exactly Like Me", "I'm One of the Smart Ones", "But the World Goes Round" and "New York, New York".

In the same year, she made her nightclub debut in Washington DC and received ecstatic reviews. Her skill as a nightclub performer grew more polished, her reputation for gaining an audience's love – and more important getting them to abandon their steaks and listen to her – was becoming quite formidable. "I'm not going for the mind, I'm not going for the groin, I'm going for the heart," Liza says. "I want to be a reflection of peoples' hearts and minds when I perform. It means I don't want to be above the public. I tried to be untouchable like Barbra Streisand and Lena Horne, but I care."

She toured the world with her increasingly accomplished act. In Paris at the Olympia she was christened *la petite Piaf americaine*; in London she held court at The Talk of the Town; in Sydney she was at The Chequers Club. Monte Carlo, New York, Las Vegas, Miami, Los Angeles. All were captive. And to each Liza brought her energy – the kind of strength-sapping adrenalin that necessitated a supply of oxygen always on hand at the side of the stage.

Her friend Mia Farrow, to whose twin sons Liza is godmother, says of Liza: "She's worked all her life but it seems there's always someone who wants to explain Liza by pulling her out of Judy's dead arms.

Opposite: Liza on stage with mother

She's nothing like Judy. She is Liza – a disciplined, well-trained and seasoned performer. She seems terribly vulnerable and she is – you have to be when every moment is new. But Liza's strong."

On March 3, 1967 after an engagement lasting two years, Liza married Peter Allen, an Australian singer her mother had discovered in a hotel in Hong Kong. It did not last, although according to Liza, Peter retained visitation rights to their dog, Ocho.

The next logical step for Liza's burgeoning prowess as a peformer was obviously films. Albert Finney had the foresight to cast her in the small but significant part of his secretary-mistress in *Charlie Bubbles*. It was an auspicious beginning but sadly, although Finney's first film as director was widely praised by the press, it was inadequately shown. Finney played the title role, that of a successful writer and Liza was his American secretary, an aspiring writer. During a trip to Manchester where old acquaintances are impressed by Charlie's material wealth, the secretary makes a clumsy attempt to seduce him. Liza's role was little more than a cameo, but although she was only on screen for perhaps twenty minutes, she made every second work. Critics called her performance "beautifully caricatured" as a cross between a snap-happy American in Europe and an eager student of "creative writing". In America where it was released first, it enjoyed a more considerable success than in Britain.

Liza's second major film was Alan J Pakula's *Pookie* (*The Sterile Cuckoo* in America). Again it was a directorial debut – until then Pakula had worked memorably with Robet Mulligan and worn the producer's hat. But directing – as this and subsequent films proved – was very much his metier. The film should have been Liza's first, since three years earlier Pakula had been all set to make it but the money was withdrawn when he insisted that Liza was the star.

The studio still were not ecstatic about the casting, but finally agreed.

Liza played Pookie Adams, a lovable kook and misfit who begins a touching and genuine relationship with a young student, Jerry Payne (movingly played by Wendell Burton). Pookie is constantly unsure of the relationship, testing its strength in many ways. To keep Jerry she tells him she is pregnant – soon however she confesses that the baby "went away". But as she has suspected all along, it is Jerry who ends the relationship. There is a shatteringly good scene when Pookie talks to Jerry on the telephone and realises that love is over. The scene lasts five minutes and was achieved in one take.

Liza's performance prompted critics to say: "she is entirely compelling, with her cropped hair, horn-rimmed glasses, toothy smile, shrill voice and breathless manner of speaking, even if much of what she says is difficult to catch. Her control is such that in two scenes in particular – on the Greyhound bus and on the telephone to Jerry – she holds our attention for minutes while Pakula just lets the camera run."

Liza's father, Vincente Minnelli, told her: "I knew you had invention but I didn't think you knew your craft so well."

Liza herself was so determined to do the film that she turned down an offer to do "Promises, Promises" on Broadway rather than let it slip away. She was nominated for an Oscar as the Best Actress of 1969 along with Genevieve Bujold (*Anne of the Thousand Days*), Jane Fonda (*They Shoot Horses, Don't They?*), Jean Simmons (*The Happy Ending*) and Maggie Smith (*The Prime of Miss Jean Brodie*). The award went to Maggie Smith.

Pakula believed, like Albert Finney, that Liza tended to show too much of her feelings in her face. Finney's advice – which she has followed faithfully ever since – was to "do half what you're doing." Pakula said Liza

Opposite: Liza the teenage singer

tended to "give too much". He remembers the experience of working with Liza as one of the happiest times of his life, mostly because of her. "One of the great delights of Liza is that she's unashamed about her need for affection and her delight in it. I find that vastly appealing in a world where everyone's proctecting themselves from being absurd and keeping their cool. I've never seen anyone get more joy out of working – and it's contagious.

It was while Liza was making her third film *Tell Me That You Love Me, Junie Moon* for Otto Preminger that Judy Garland died of an accidental overdose of sleeping pills (the coroner's verdict). "When she died I almost knew why," says Liza. "She let her guard down. She didn't die from an overdose. I think she just got tired. She lived like a taut wire. I don't think she ever looked for real happiness, because she always thought happiness would mean the end."

Preminger recalls Liza's strength and how she coped with everything. "The way she behaved during those trying days and took care of all the arrangements was really an inspiration to watch," Preminger said. Liza was calm while the world mourned vocally. "Elevator men were falling around me weeping," Liza says. "I was the only one standing up. I got so mad at everybody. I remember yelling at someone – 'You cried for her when she sang "Over the Rainbow" and "The Man That Got Away". Now at last she's at peace. Smile, for God's sake!' "

But in a curious way Liza Minnelli could only begin to forge her own legend after her mother died. It was after Judy died that people finally gave Liza credit for being, not Judy Garland's daughter, but Liza Minnelli, a unique entertainer in her own right. The comparison would continue; Liza has long since resigned herself to that. But Judy's death allowed Liza to be her own person. "My father gave me my dreams, Mama gave me my drive," she acknowledges.

Tell Me That You Love Me, Junie Moon would probably have been a difficult film to make even without Liza having to cope with Judy's death in the middle of it. After the caring relationship she had enjoyed with the previous directors, briefly with Albert Finney, more thoroughly with Alan Pakula, Otto Preminger was a new experience. Liza had already won a one-picture deal, almost unheard of from Preminger who liked to have options on his leading players. "Otto Preminger's theory is that the actor is hired to act, and he must be ready at all times," Liza explained. "He wants the work done immediately and perfectly. You get the impression with Otto that you don't have time to ask questions, and you come in and don't ask, and if you do it wrong, you get yelled at. It's like teachers. There are some who correct you by saying, 'It would be better this way', and others who just say, 'That's *wrong*'. And Otto is the latter."

The film told of the relationship between three hopelessly maladjusted young people – Junie Moon, permanently disfigured after her deranged boyfriend deliberately spilled acid on her face; Warren, a homosexual paraplegic; Arthur, an introverted epileptic. These three meet in hospital and decide to set up house together after they are released. The film was very sketchily released: some felt it was in bad taste, others felt you could not possibly take the "love conquers all" theme, or its luckless characters, seriously. In the Independent Film Journal, Lloyd Ibert said: "Liza Minnelli who, if she plays her career cards right, will become one of the greatest actresses of the '70s, is never given any opportunity to build a characterisation with all those wham bam scenes flying by. But her agonised cry when she discovers her lover has died in her arms suggests what *Junie Moon* as a film should have achieved." In Britain, John Trevelyan, then the censor, asked for the removal of some frames where Junie writhes on the ground following the acid attack. "You are a butcher," Otto Preminger is said to have stormed. "And you, you are a sadist," Trevelyan replied stoically.

Liza cornered her share of the praise: "Much of the credit must go to Liza Minnelli's assured performance and the admirable support she received from Ken Howard and Robert Moore." But, the review continued in less complimentary fashion: "The jokes and the tricks are obviously intended to lighten the load but the whole thing is impossible to take seriously anyway, with Junie dispensing just the right psychological therapy for a nervous disorder, and Warren, magically cured of a lifetime of homosexuality by a night on the beach with a lady intellectual, rebuking a reference to his prowess in the kitchen with a petulant, 'I'm not making brownies any more – ever'."

Otto Preminger remained faithful in his support of Liza. "I think she is giving a remarkable performance, and will move with this picture into the front rank of actors and stars." Liza commented: "I can identify with ugly people. Sometimes my own ugliness overwhelms me."

But Liza's biggest challenge was just ahead: *Cabaret*. In this film the full impact of Liza Minnelli's talent was felt, probably for the first time. Certainly the potential for a performance such as this was evident from her earlier work but its realisation was more impressive than even her most devoted fans could have hoped.

Liza had auditioned for the role of Sally Bowles on Broadway – she says she auditioned fourteen times, but other sources say that the producers were set on an English girl playing Sally and seeing Liza was a mere formality before Jill Haworth was given the part. Whatever the truth, Liza had been obsessed by Sally Bowles for a long time. "I saw Julie Harris play

Sally in *I am a Camera* and she was great, but she played her like a campy butterfly who was scatter-brained. I saw Sally as a girl with an element of terrible selfishness and meanness. She really is a tramp, not just another lovable kook. Sally doesn't want to be good, she just wants to be a star. And she's a girl who improvises her whole life and her fantasy of tomorrow is so strong that she really can't take a good look at now."

Of the Broadway cast of "Cabaret" only Joel Grey was invited to recreate his decadent Master of Ceremonies in the screen version. Grey says of Liza, "She is capable of making you care about her, making you want to protect her – and then you realise that she's perfectly capable of protecting herself."

As Sally Bowles, the "divinely decadent" singer at the Kit Kat Klub, Liza was superb. The source of *Cabaret* was Christopher Isherwood's "Goodbye to Berlin" which became the film *I Am A Camera*. This became a musical play "Cabaret" with book by Joe Masteroff, music by John Kander and lyrics by Fred Ebb. The screenplay for the film was by Jay Presson Allen. It was set in the Berlin of the 1930s. Sally Bowles is a singer at the Kit Kat Klub, a romantic girl yearning for stardom and dreaming of being taken way from "all this".

All this is the tawdry, third-rate world where money is king and the Nazi presence is rapidly making its mark. Into Sally's life comes Brian Roberts (a generous, self-effacing performance by Michael York), a young English graduate who hopes to improve his German by living in Berlin. Sally and Brian have rooms in the same boarding house and become friends. Brian's ambivalent sexuality, his admission that his previous relationships with girls have been disastrous, does not stop them finally drifting into a sexual relationship. It is not a success. Sally finds another man, Baron Maximilian von Heune, who showers her and Brian

Opposite: a portrait taken at the time of Tell Me That You Love Me, Julie Moon

with presents and entertains them at his country home.

Sally admits to Brian that she and Max are lovers and Brian confesses that he, too, has shared Max's bed. When Sally becomes pregnant, Brian offers to marry her, but she secretly has an abortion. Brian leaves Berlin, older and wiser for having lived there, and Sally stays on waiting for the big break. "Most people are like Sally," says Liza. "She very much represents her era. She tries desperately to be original and enjoys shocking people. She's also selfish and childish. Sally was a mosaic that took a long time for me to find. At first she was like branches that have no form. Sally desperately wants to be a movie star. I studied hundreds of photographs of movie stars in the '30s. Gradually I came to know this girl I was playing – what kind of person she was, what motivated her actions, and how she would react to specific situations."

Cabaret was director Bob Fosse's second film (his first was *Sweet Charity*) and established him as a creative, sensitive director, capable of wringing every ounce of emotion out of a scene, while avoiding mawkish sentimentality which could so easily have overtaken it. Liza commented: "My hardest scene was the very first dialogue sequence. We had been filming a musical number, and right in the middle was an important scene I had with Michael York and Helmut Griem, I went blank and into a panic. I felt I wasn't ready. That's when Bob Fosse came over and said, 'Don't worry, Liza, it's only a bit of film'. I relaxed immediately and the scene went well."

The film won excellent reviews: critics unaccustomed to glowing superlatives suddenly found themselves unanimously enthusiastic. "Liza Minnelli, with her strange waif-like looks and elfin sexuality, is perfectly cast as Sally Bowles, and the objection that she is evidently too good to be performing in some tatty

cabaret seems pretty academic," said John Russell Taylor.

When the Academy Awards were announced, *Cabaret* was nominated in ten categories. Liza was nominated as Best Actress in competition with Diana Ross (*Lady Sings the Blues*), Maggie Smith (*Travels With My Aunt*), Cicely Tyson (*Sounder*) and Liv Ullman (*The Emigrants*). *Cabaret* was nominated for Best Film, Best Director (Bob Fosse), Best Supporting Actor (Joel Grey), Best Sceenplay based on material from another medium, Best Art Direction (Rolf Zehetbauer and Jugen Kiebach), Best Set Direction (Herbert Strabl), Best Cinematography (Geoffrey Unsworth), Best Sound (Robert Knudson and David Hildyard), Best Editing (David Bretherton), Best Scoring (adapted by Ralph Burns).

The biggest surprise when the Awards were announced was Liza winning Best Actress (the film itself only failed to win Best Film and Best Screenplay). Diana Ross and Cicely Tyson were both nominated and the feeling was running high that it would be the year when the Award would go to a black actress.

Liza had a three year wait for a script that excited her sufficiently to sign a contract. "I kept getting scripts but all of them seemed to have me waiting in the alley while the fellow was off chasing someone. 'Listen,' I said, 'why can't the guy stand in the alley sometimes? I'm good at chasing people'." Meanwhile she appeared in nightclubs and cabaret and made a magnificent television special "Liza With a Z" directed by Bob Fosse which was screened by NBC on September 10, 1972, and became an Emmy award winner.

Liza's emotional maturity suffered a set back in 1973 when she arrived in Britain for three concerts at the London Palladium and met Peter Sellers. Sensing a story, the press pursued them. Eventually Liza called a press conference at the Savoy Hotel (Peter Sellers was making *Soft Beds, Hard Battles* at Shepperton Studios). "I fell in love with this man and I am pleased to say that he fell in love with me," she announced. It signalled the end of her engagement to Desi Arnaz Jnr, seven years her junior. Then after five hectic weeks the romance with Sellers was over: she returned to America and Peter went back to the set. Meanwhile in America producer Jack Haley Jnr was compiling *That's Entertaiment* from the MGM archives. "I was screening all the marvellous Judy Garland–Mickey Rooney films and suddenly thought that Liza was the logical person to narrate that segment. What could have been more natural? Who could have done it better?" Liza was at the time enjoying a triumphant, record breaking engagement with her one woman show at New York's vast Winter Garden, plunging her energies wholeheartedly into her favourite role as an entertainer – and winning her second Tony award in the process. But she agreed to narrate the Judy Garland sequence of *That's Entertainment*. Jack Haley Jnr is the son of the man who played The Tin Man in *The Wizard of Oz* opposite Judy Garland. The implications were lost on nobody, and it seemed right that, in Haley, Liza would find the stability she needed. They were married September 17, 1974 and spent their honeymoon in England promoting *That's Entertainment*.

Liza reckoned the film was the best tribute to her mother ever made. "My father says that what Jack has done in the film is help us remember the sections of the past that we want to remember. Nostalgia is really the way you think it was. That's where I think he's been so clever: he's really made a new film because he's used the best clips. Some of the films which surrounded those clips were terribly boring. I remember sitting through some of them and honestly,

by the time they came to the one good number you were so bored that someone could have walked on the water and all you'd think was, 'Fine, now let me go home'."

She seemed to be content to be Mrs Jack Haley. "If somebody loves you, they give you their name. It's about all they've got in the long run. I believe in tradition. I was born in tradition. My parents were very romantic. With Jack it's possible for me to lead a very private life where it wasn't when I was on my own. He's a marvellous man. When I met him he said, 'You've got a pretty hot reputation, haven't you?' So I looked right back and said, 'So have you'. He'd always been seen around the blondes with marvellous figures, you see. A while back he talked to Sophia Loren and she told him, 'So at last you got smart and married a nice brown-haired Italian girl'."

Liza returned to Broadway in 1975 to replace an ailing Gwen Verdon in "Chicago", rehearsing for just a week before her run of standing room only performances began. Since then she has returned again and again to the possibility of filming "Chicago", something she is clearly intent upon doing.

Liza's three year wait for the right film script ended when she signed to make *Lucky Lady* for director Stanley Donen. Writers Willard Huyck and Gloria Katz were hired at an enormous fee to concoct a sure-fire hit. It would be a three-hander: Liza Minnelli, Gene Hackman, Burt Reynolds. The formula they built followed the adventures of three partners trafficking in illegal boose during Prohibition. Their transport? A ketch called Lucky Lady. These three independent souls buck the system, outwit the coast guard and the Establishment runners who take the sport and romance out of trafficking, but retribution does come. It worked excellently during the early scenes but the sudden

*Opposite: in
Lucky Lady*

switch from lightest comedy and frolic to pathos jolted the film into a different direction. So uncertain were the film makers that Donen shot three endings and the fantasy ending was most widely used, to the chagrin of the stars who verbally complained during the press junkets organised by 20th Century-Fox. It was a difficult film to make and Liza remembers being cooped on the ketch for hours at a stretch for weeks on end: sixty-five people on a boat intended for a mere dozen. The film did not provide the box office bonanza expected of it.

For many years Liza's personal ambition was to work with her father. They talked of making a film about Scott Fitzgerald's wife Zelda. "It's the energy levels in the characters I pick that attact me," said Liza. "I don't want to talk about Zelda being crazy, because that's not what's good about her. She was chasing life. She wanted to do something, she had incredible drive. She didn't give up." Sadly, those plans came to nothing, but then along came *A Matter of Time*, based on the novel "Film of Memory" by former French Minister of Culture, Maurice Druon.

"I've been begging Daddy since I was five to put me in one of his films but he kept saying, 'Wait.' I was getting insecure: I thought he didn't consider me good enough to work with him." Vincente Minnelli had wanted to film the novel for ten years but only gained access to the rights in 1973. He sent Liza a script. "It had me hooked from the start," she says.

The story concerns a simple Italian village girl (Liza) who works as a chambermaid in a once fashionable, now run-down hotel in Rome. There she is befriended by an elderly impoverished Contessa (Ingrid Bergman) whose wit, beauty, and sophistication once made her the toast of Europe. Hearing the old lady's stories, the maid fantasises the past with herself as the Contessa.

Once again Oscar-winning cinematographer

Opposite: in one of the numbers from Lucky Lady

GeoffreyUnsworth was engaged to light the picture, his third with Liza (the others were *Cabaret* and *Lucky Lady*). "Nobody ever photographs me the way Geoffrey did," Liza enthused. The regard was mutual.

Liza followed *A Matter of Time* with a guest appearance as herself in Mel Brooks' hilarious comedy *Silent Movie*, about a group of movie makers gathering together a cast of superstars for their silent picture which will save the studio from the wicked machinations of Engulf and Devour, a company intent on a takeover bid. Among the other stars who played themselves in *Silent Movie* were James Caan, Burt Reynolds, Anne Bancroft, Marcel Marceau and Paul Newman.

She was then reunited with John Kander and Fred Ebb for a musical love story of the post World War II years as, *New York, New York*, directed by arguably the most impressive of the new directors, Martin Scorsese (*Alice Doesn't Live Here Anymore, Taxi Driver*) and co-starring Robert DeNiro (*Godfather II, Taxi Driver, The Last Tycoon*). Liza plays a small time band vocalist promoted by DeNiro's saxophone player, but she quickly eclipses him both in talent and in public appeal. Instead of splitting selflessly, they are wedged apart by the acrimony that follows in the wake of her career success. Years later, playing to an elite supper club audience after her own Hollywood success, she acknowledges his help and influence by performing the song ("New York, New York") that he wrote for her.

"The musicals of the late '40s and early '50s were entrenched in a cloud cuckooland of escapist fantasy. In his deliberate homage one might expect Martin Scorsese to have cut a swath through this crop of sentimental whimsy. But although there are moments of blunt, savage realism and unassailable truth in all Scorsese's films, a realist is the last thing you would

Opposite: on location in Rome for A Matter of Time

call him ... It is no more a realistic musical than *Taxi Driver* was a realistic vigilante story ... Yet it is a film full of music: not only the drilling tool of Liza Minnelli's wondrously full-throated voice, nor yet that melancholy saxophone that Robert DeNiro mimes to ... *New York, New York* has superb performances from its two prinicipals, DeNiro's contribution perhaps being the greater in that he makes sympathetic a character of considerable unattractiveness. Minnelli's vocabulary or nervous giggles and swallowed sobs hasn't been better used since *Cabaret* and her singing style has the fullness and soul-felt ache of the mature Judy Garland," said David Castell in Films Illustrated.

There was one edit of the troubled *New York, New York* that pleased director Martin Scorsese. Unfortunately it ran four hours and twenty-nine minutes and, bewitched as he was by his creation, even Scorsese saw that it would not be commercially viable. He cut it to two hours and forty-five minutes, reshooting scenes that had been affected by the severity of the editing. This version was further reduced to two hours and twenty-two minutes and United Artists cut a further fifteen minutes before opening the film in the United Kingdom. In 1981 a longer version of the film was re-issued in Britain.

New York, New York failed to work the magic trick of *Cabaret*, though it has many individual champions. Perhaps the idea of Minnelli and DeNiro in the big band era seemed old hat to the increasingly unpredictable public taste. However, two numbers at least have become standard Minnelli vehicles – "New York, New York" and "But the World Goes Round", written by John Kander and Fred Ebb.

By this time Liza's marriage to Jack Haley was in deep trouble and her name was being linked with, among others, Mikhail Baryshnikov the brilliant Russian ballet dancer, Gower Champion the choreographer

Opposite: in Martin Scorses's New York, New York

and director, and Martin Scorsese. The rumours persisted when Scorsese directed her in the Broadway musical "The Act". Despite some appalling notices, this show rapidly became the hottest ticket in town and Liza was certainly the best thing in it and won her third Tony award for it. Dance critic Walter Terry in The Saturday Review said: "Miss Minnelli, however celebrated she may be as a singer, is most certainly a dancer, and an exceptionally good one. Even when she is simply singing, she almost always embroiders the song with danced gesture."

During her stint in "The Act" Liza also pursued a vigorous party life and this led to a near collapse and hospitalisation on one occasion, and many missed nights. When she wasn't performing, there was no show, since she was the reason audiences came in the first place. Jack Haley tried to quell rumours on the domestic front while Liza angrily declared: "The gossips are trying to ruin us. I love my husband and all this talk about me going off with other men is driving me mad. I loathe it all."

Said her loyal agent, explaining that Liza needed rest because of the ravages of her illness and the fact that her solo performance in "The Act" drained so much from her: "Liza is fantastically dedicated and professional in every sense of the word. She would never be late or miss a show unless she was in dire health straits. Her husband and everyone else who loves her dearly hope that a few days in hospital will give her back her health and energy. She is too beautiful a person to suffer like this."

Liza's interest in dance led in the summer of 1979 to her narating the ballet "The Owl and the Pussycat" for the Martha Graham Dance Company at the Metropolitan Opera House, a production Liza also followed to London. While in London she took time out to guest star on "The Muppet Show" and it seemed appropriate that one of the greatest

Opposite: with Judy Garland on set at MGM

entertainers on earth should work on the most successful television show on earth. She starred in two dance orientated television specials, the first "Goldie and Liza: Together" paired her with Goldie Hawn; the second "Baryshnikov on Broadway" became a memorable trip through America's hit musicals with the legendary Mikhail Baryshnikov. "Misha just loves that Broadway razzmatazz," Liza said. "They don't have a lot of it in Russia." Both shows were huge hits worldwide and won Emmys. The Baryshnikov programme won the Golden Rose at the prestigious Montreux Festival.

Liza was the first performer ever to sell out a full week of Carnegie Hall concerts, and she continues to dominate whatever work area she chooses. "I couldn't do it all if I didn't love it," she says. "Work is being around people who are smarter than you are, and learning. The brain is an erogenous zone as far as I'm concerned. I love the creative process." (As one writer observed: "She lives on a diet of fingernails and a kind of drive and excitement for show business that is almost scaring.") Her one woman shows at the London Palladium in 1978 were sold out within hours of tickets going on sale – despite the fact that seat prices were way in excess of the Palladium norm.

On December 4, 1979 Liza married French speaking Mark Gero who she met when he stage managed "The Act". Her marriage to Jack Haley had been dissolved a year earlier. Six years her junior, the staggeringly good looking Gero is variously described as "Broadway producer" and "sculptor". The ceremony took place at St Bartholomews Episcopal Church in New York and was attended by Elizabeth Taylor and other chic friends. Designer Halson flew back from Washington to supervise the final details of Liza's wrap-around dusty pink chiffon wedding dress and it was at his home off Park Avenue that the reception was held – strictly family and close friends only.

Less than two weeks later Liza was rushed to hospital where she miscarried the baby she and Mark Gero were expecting. It was a bitter blow to the maternity obsessed Liza.

The couple settled down at an apartment in Central Park South where Liza insisted she wasn't a party person at all, much preferring quiet evenings at home reading books, playing her guitar, and watching television. "People seem to think that because I played the messed-up Sally Bowles, then that's how I must be in real life. I don't take my life to the limit. I enjoy my life and value it. If I'd lived the life I was supposed to, I'd be in a bottle at a research centre. I don't have a tumultuous private life. When I go to a party, it's a good one, and that's the one everyone is watching."

Meanwhile she bemoaned the paucity of the scripts she was being offered. "I haven't done any films recently because there haven't been any scripts that I like. I stopped doing films because I was bored with them." Then, just when she was despairing, along came *Arthur*. "I read the script, found out that Dudley Moore and Sir John Gielgud were going to be in it and I said, 'That's for me'."

Arthur is a contemporary love story about a little rich man (Dudley Moore) – heir to a £400 million fortune who is forced to become engaged to a sweet young debutante. Then he falls in love with a zany Italian girl (Liza) he finds shoplifting in a big store. ("She's not really a shoplifter," Liza Minnelli says in defence of Linda Marolla, the character she plays in *Arthur*. "She's a waitress and acting student who wants to give her out-of-work father something special for his birthday.").

Apparently, making the film was unmitigated joy. "Dudley and I work well together," Liza said. "We make each other laugh."

Dudley Moore returned the compliment: "Stage

actors, like myself and Liza appreciate that you have to go on every night at eight, ready or not. None of this waiting until you're in just the right mood and frame of mind. Of course, when you're around Liza it's easy to be in a good mood. Her confidence attracts people."

Liza said: "I grew up around celebrities, not like some name performers who are freaked by their fame. Those people, you don't just walk up and grab. But I'm the kind of person people do come up to and touch. They treat me more like I'm their kid, for some reason."

Arthur director Steve Gordon, who also wrote the screenplay, confirms this. "People visiting the set fell down laughing at Dudley but they wanted to reach out and touch Liza. It's as if some bit of her magic would rub off on them."

In blistering New York summer heat, they filmed in the streets, becoming a tourist attraction for passers-by. One brief sequence took nine takes, the best of which was blown when someone in a passing van shouted through a window: "Hey, are you people making a movie?"

Liza was unfazed. "Some actors complain about retakes, but when you've done a lot of stage work, you accept that repetition is the key to getting inside a character."

Dudley Moore agreed. "I like repetition. Eating is repetitious. Sex is repetitious. Waking up in the morning is repetitious. Things which aren't repetitious are apt to be dangerous, like swimming in shark infested waters or doing your own stunts."

The film became the surprise hit of 1981 breaking box office records all over America and remaining top of Variety's hot hundred films for many months.

While she was making *Arthur*, Liza talked excitedly about her determination to have a baby. "I want to have a baby as soon as I can. It wouldn't mean the end

Opposite: as Sally Bowles in Bob Fosse's Cabaret

of my career but I would certainly take a year off. I think it's important not to miss the first year of my child's life. I've been out kicking my legs too long. My business is fantasy. You're a fool to take it for anything else."

While waiting and hoping, Liza did voluntary work with handicapped children. "I work a lot with brain damaged children. There's a marvellous place up in Philadelphia where I work two weeks a year. I'm also on the board of directors."

Apparently it was largely the effect of working with Goldie Hawn, who became a close friend, and being around Goldie's children, that reawakened Liza's desire for motherhood. "Goldie talked about how much fun it was to be pregnant and convinced me that having children is a very important experience. To produce a new human being must be the greatest thing a woman can do. Films may flop, critics may groan, but a child is there forever."

Goldie Hawn played down her contribution: "Liza obviously had a lot of fun with my kids. She became great buddies with them. I just told her I thought having children was the most beautiful, important thing a woman does in her life."

In October 1980 Liza discovered she was pregnant and, following doctors orders, she cancelled work and took to her bed, à la Sophia Loren and Audrey Hepburn. But it was not to be. Early in January 1981, despite corrective surgery, Liza miscarried.

In March 1981 she was back at work: concerts with Joel Grey, her *Cabaret* co-star, and tours with her one woman show, and talk of a film with John Travolta as well as the renewed speculation about a film version of "Chicago".

Inevitably there has been talk that Liza will one day portray her mother on film. "Never," she says. And that her father will direct such a film. "Never," says Vincente Minnelli. Similarly, when Liza is asked to sing "Over the Rainbow" her response is quiet, self contained and quite definite. "It's been sung," she says.

She is highly strung, affectionate and warm, child-like one moment, adult the next. But when you consider her background that is scarcely surprising. "Everyone used to tell me their problems; it was really funny. But I wasn't a kid then. I don't really remember having any childhood. I always had responsibilities and never felt free until I was twenty. Then I thought,'This is ridiculous. I'm going to be a kid for a while'."

She inspires enormous loyalty and love. Among those who adore her are actors, singers and fans. Charles Aznavour, with whom she made a television special claims a relationship with Liza similar to the one he shared with Edith Piaf. "It's less than love and more than friendship. It's better than romance."

Director Alan J Pakula says: "To see someone who has the knowledge of pain and the great capacity for joy is one of the great audience experiences, and Liza

This page: choreographer Danny Daniels rehearses Liza and company for the show Best Foot Forward

Opposite: with Albert Finney in Charlie Bubbles

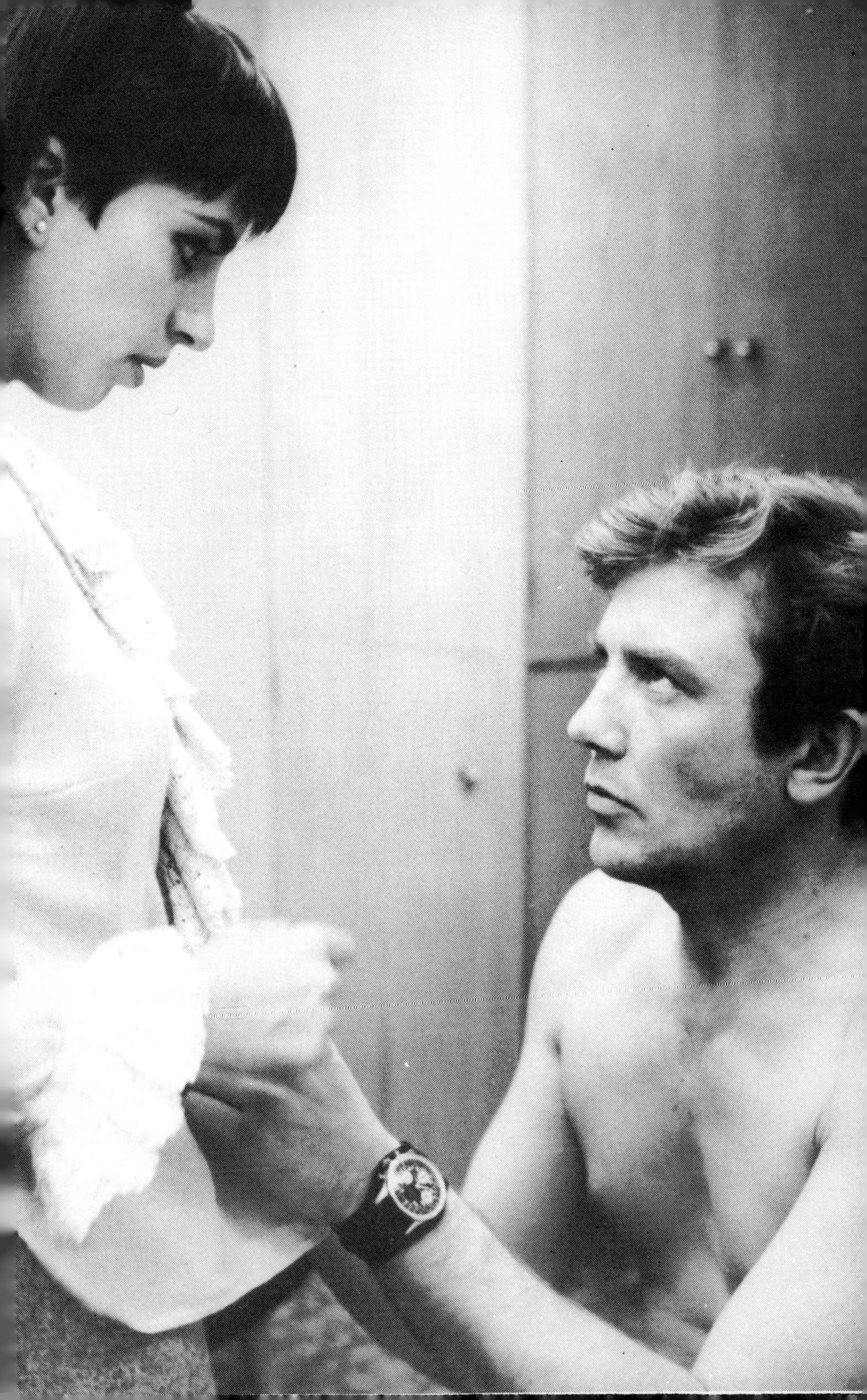

can convey as much as anybody I've ever known. Her range will be dictated very much by what happens to her as a woman. But however much she grows up and has grown up, I hope she never loses that unguarded quality. There are many things an actress can learn, but the ability to create life in a character is something you have or you don't have. That's the talent Liza has."

Liza avoids talking too much about the past. "I love gossip and reading about other people's pasts. But I don't like talking about my own. People are always asking – what was it like? But the past is finished for me. I lived it. So I can't think why it should be so interesting."

Whatever she tackles next she has a wealth of professionalism and experience to offer; a bank of expertise whether as actress, singer or nightclub entertainer. "Becoming an actress is an extension of childhood because you have the opportunity of living out your fantasies and making them come true.

This page: congratulations on the second night of Flora the Red Menace from father Vincente and mother Judy Garland

Opposite: with Albert Finney in Charlie Bubbles

PORTRAIT GALLERY

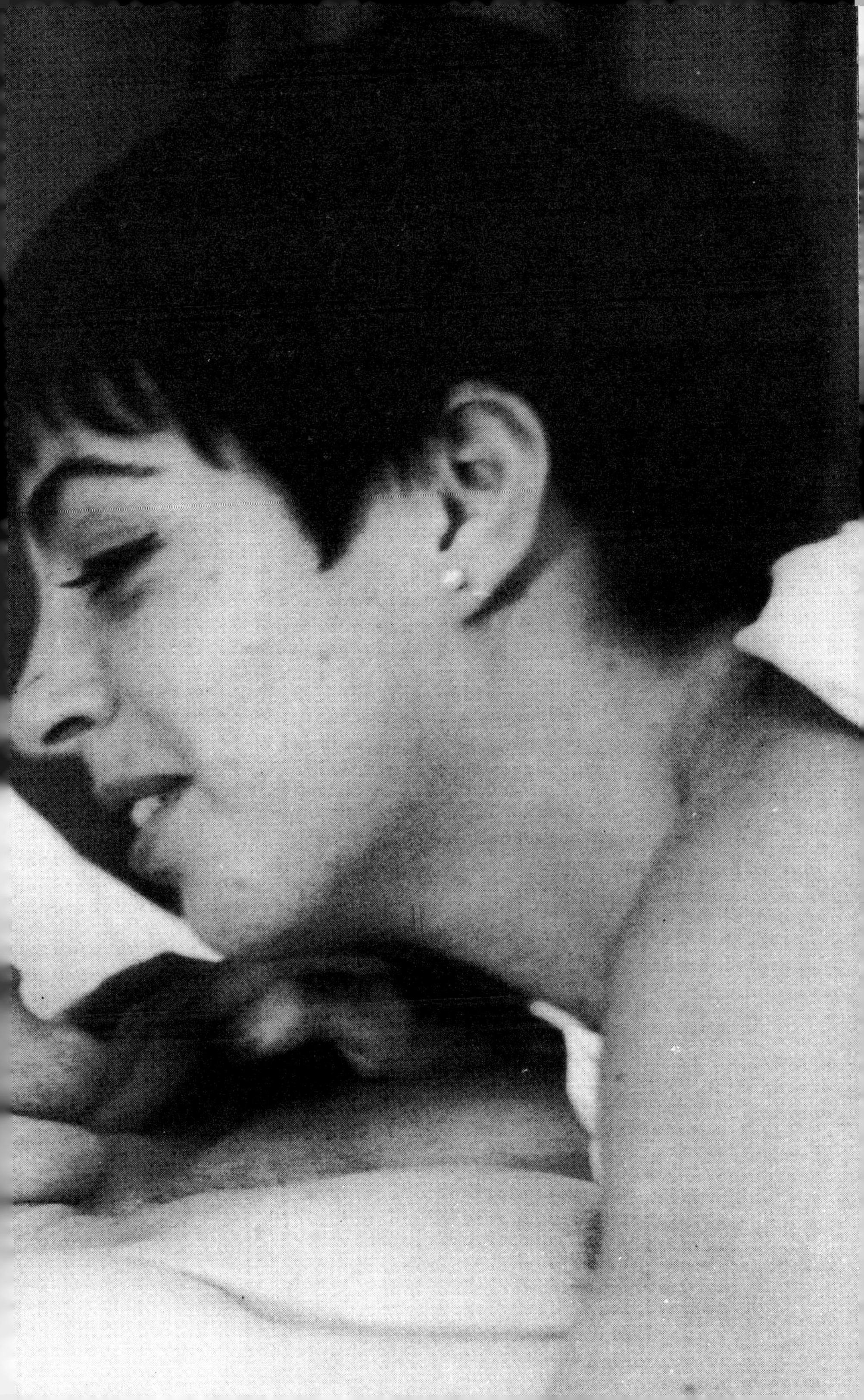

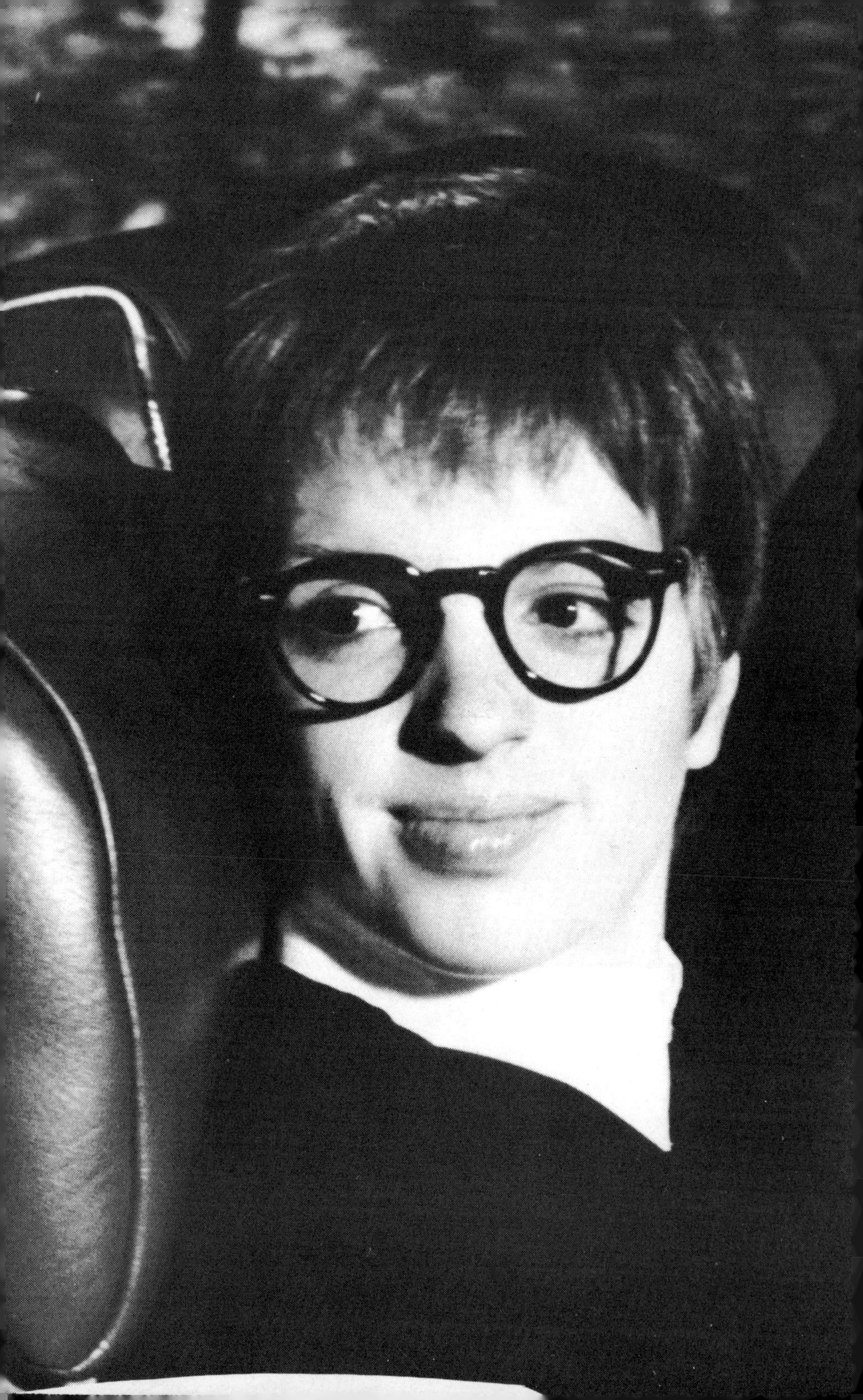

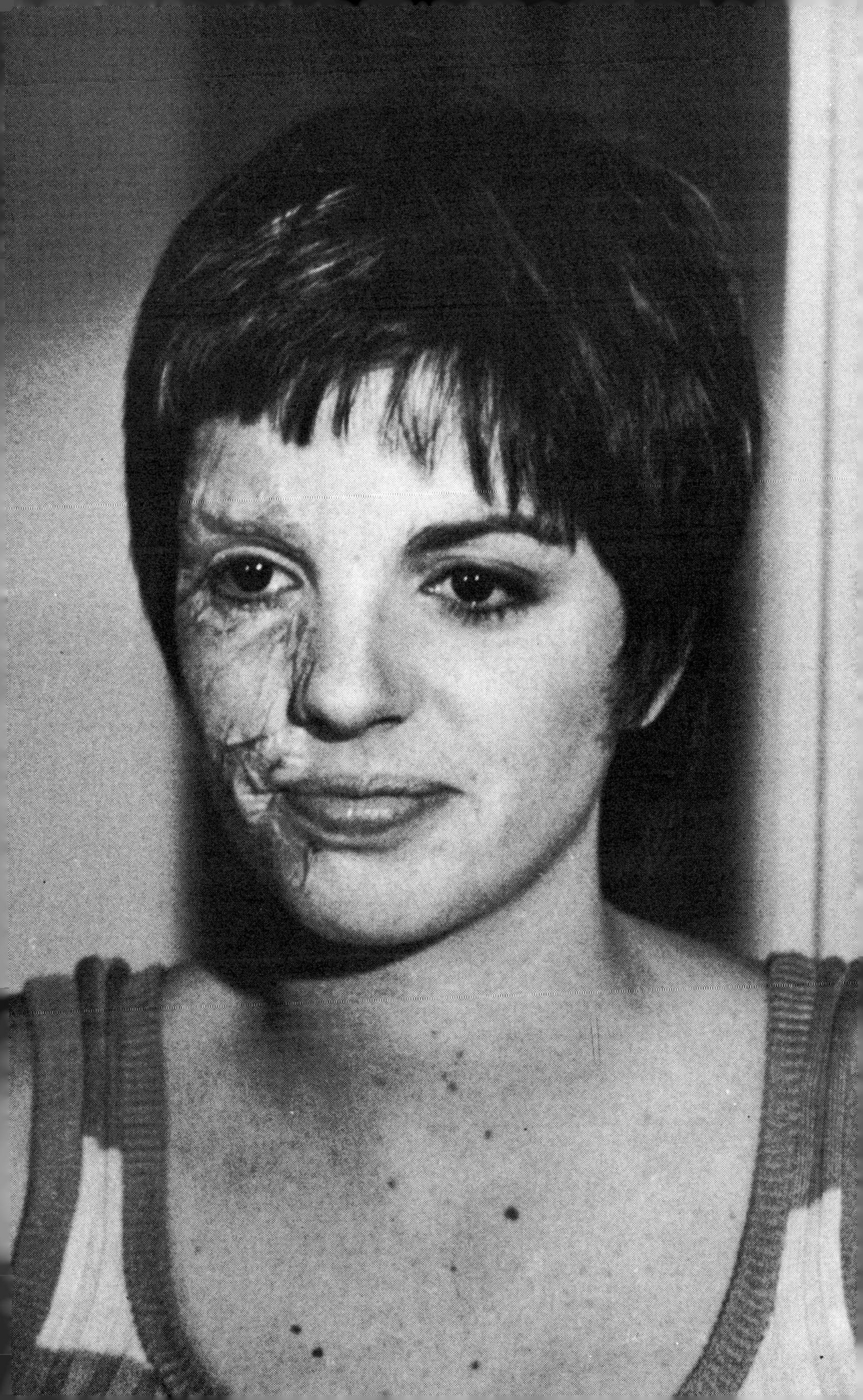

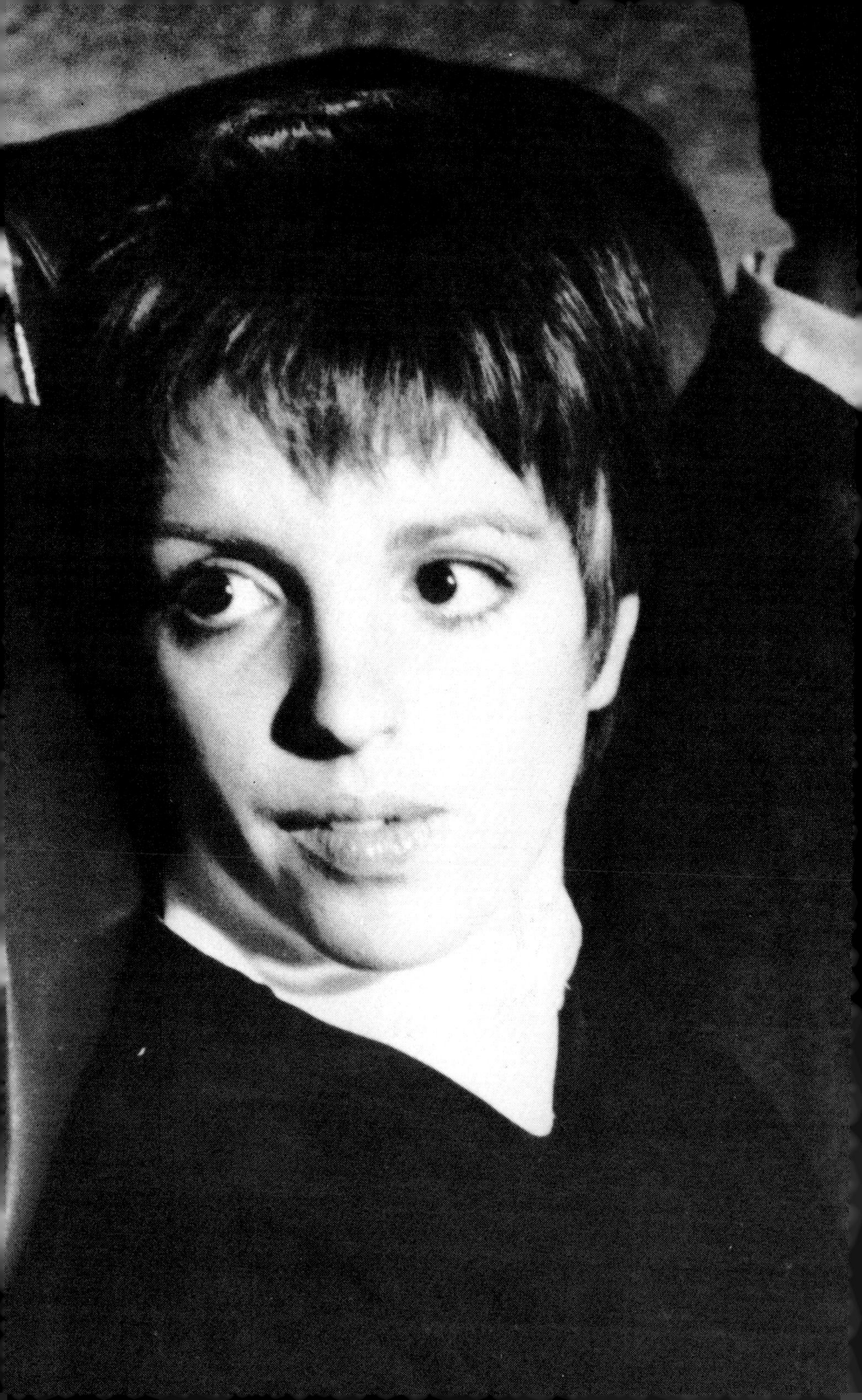

IN THE GOOD OLD SUMMERTIME (US 1949)
Prod/Joe Pasternak. Dir/Robert Z Leonard. Scr/Albert
Hackett, Frances Goodrich, Ivan Tors, based on the play by
Miklos Laszlo. Music/Robert Alton. Ph/Harry Stradling.
Technicolor. GB distribution/CIC (MGM). Certificate U.
103 mins.
With: Judy Garland (Veronica Fisher), Van Johnson
(Andrew Delby Larkin), S Z Sakall (Otto Oberkrugen),
Spring Byington (Nellie Burke), Clinton Sunberg (Rudy
Hansen), Buster Keaton (Hickey), Marcia Van Dyke (Louise
Parkson)
Liza Minnelli, an adorable two year old, had her first screen
appearance in the finale of this romantic MGM musical
starring Judy Garland and Van Johnson.

JOURNEY BACK TO OZ (US 1962)
Prod/Norman Prescott, Lou Scheimer. Dir/Hal Sutherland.
Scr/Fred Ladd, Norman Prescott, from a book by L Frank
Baum. Music/Sammy Cahn. Ph/Sergio Antonio. Eastman
Colour. GB distribution/Columbia-Warner (Warner).
Certificate U. 88 mins.
With the voices of: Liza Minnelli (Dorothy), Mickey Rooney

*Opposite: with
Robert DeNiro in
New York, New
York*

(The Scarecrow), Danny Thomas (The Tin Man), Milton Berle (The Cowardly Lion), Ethel Merman (Old Mombi), Paul Lynde (Jack Pumpkinhead), Herscel Bernardi (Woodenhead, the Saw Horse), Rise Stevens (Glinda the Good), Margaret Hamilton (Aunt Em), Paul Ford (Uncle Henry)

Liza's screen career seemed in jeopardy of never being realised, with her second appearance during a wedding sequence in her father's film, *The Long, Long Trailer* (1954) ending on the cutting room floor. In *Journey Back to Oz*, an animated sequel to *Wizard of Oz*, Liza took her mother's role and became the voice over for a cartoon version of Dorothy. The film was made in 1962, but not released until 1974, a full twelve years later.

CHARLIE BUBBLES (GB 1967)
Prod/Michael Medwin. Dïr/Albert Finney. Scr/Shelagh Delaney. Music/Misha Donat. Ph/Peter Suschitsky. Technicolor. GB distribution/Rank. Certificate X. 89 mins. With: Albert Finney (Charlie Bubbles), Billie Whitelaw (Lottie), Colin Blakely (Smokey Pickles), Liza Minnelli (Eliza), Timothy Garland (Jack), Richard Pearson

(Accountant), John Ronane (Gerry), Nicholas Phipps (Agent), Peter Sallis (Lawyer), Charles Lamb (Mr Noseworthy), Margery Mason (Mrs Noseworthy), Diana Coupland (Maud), Alan Lake (Airman), Yootha Joyce (Woman in a motorway cafe)

This film acted as a double debut, for Liza Minnelli as an adult actress and for Albert Finney as a director. Though hardly a pivotal character in the film, Liza's role as Eliza was considered by many to be the highpoint of Finney's offbeat movie about a wealthy writer returning to his hometown of Manchester. As Eliza, Liza was cast as a somewhat naive young American girl, whose attraction to Finney's character of author Charlie Bubbles was that of an aspiring modern writer who would do anything for a successful author, acting as secretary, companion, lover, in hope of gaining vaulable experience for her career. Charlie Bubbles proved to be more interested in taking whatever he could from Eliza, either oblivious or uncaring about her own desires.

THE STERILE CUCKOO (GB: POOKIE) (US 1969)
Prod-dir/Alan J Pakula. Scr/Alvin Sargent, based on the novel by John Nichols. Music/Fred Karlin. Song "Come

Saturday Morning" by Fred Karlin, Dore Previn, and sung by The Sandpipers. Ph/Milton R Krasner. Technicolor. GB distribution/CIC (Paramount). Certificate X. 107 mins.
With: Liza Minnelli (Pookie Adams), Wendell Burton (Jerry Payne), Tim McIntire (Charlie Schumacher), Elizabeth Harrower (Landlady), Austin Green (Pookie's father), Sandra Faison (Nancy Putnam)
Liza Minnelli plays the lonely young Pookie Adams, in this film which takes a successfully honest look at the sensitive feelings of young lovers. A sad story in which Pookie starts the relationship with naive young student Jerry Payne (Wendell Burton), a college freshman, only to see him mature and drift further away from her until he finally outgrows her.

TELL ME THAT YOU LOVE ME JUNIE MOON (US 1969)
Prod-dir/Otto Preminger. Scr/Marjorie Kellogg, based on her novel. Music/Philip Springer. Songs "Old Devil Time" written & sung by Pete Seeger, "The Rake" and "Work Your Show" by Philip Springer, Estelle Levitt, "Elvira" written & sung by Pacific Gas and Electric. Ph/Boris Kaufman. Technicolor. GB distribution/CIC (Paramount). Certificate X. 113 mins.

With: Liza Minnelli (Junie Moon), Ken Howard (Arthur), Robert Moore (Warren), James Coco (Mario), Kay Thompson (Miss Gregory), Fred Williams (Beach boy)
Another strongly emotional film starring Liza Minnelli, considered to be one of Preminger's best. As Junie Moon, Liza played a hopelessly maladjusted girl, whose face had been hideously and permanently scarred. With a wheelchair-bound homosexual and an incredibly shy epileptic, she sets up house when they leave hospital, hoping the three of them can lead normal lives.

CABARET (US 1972)

Prod/Cy Feuer. Dir/Bob Fosse. Scr/Jay Presson Allen, based on the musical play by Joe Masteroft (book), John Kander (music), Fred Ebb (lyrics), based on the play "I Am A Camera" by John Van Druten, adapted from the book "Goodbye to Berlin" by Christopher Isherwood. Choreography/Bob Fosse. Ph/Geoffrey Unsworth. Technicolor. GB distribution/20th Century-Fox. Certificate X. 123 mins.
With: Liza Minnelli (Sally Bowles), Michael York (Brian

This page: with Robert DeNiro in New York, New York

Opposite: in New York, New York

Roberts), Helmut Griem (Maximilian von Heune), Joel Grey (Master of Ceremonies), Fritz Wepper (Fritz Wendel), Marisa Berenson (Natalie Landauer)

THAT'S ENTERTAINMENT (US 1974)
Prod-dir-scr/Jack Haley Jnr. Music/Henry Mancini. Ph/Gene Polito, Ernest Laszlo, Russell Metty, Ennio Guarnieri, Allan Green. Metrocolor. GB distribution/CIC. Certificate U. 137 mins.
With: Fred Astaire, Bing Crosby, Gene Kelly, Peter Lawford, Liza Minnelli, Donald O'Connor, Debbie Reynolds, Mickey Rooney, Frank Sinatra, James Stewart, Elizabeth Taylor
A logical choice to narrate the Judy Garland segment, Liza lent her voice to this compilation movie of over 100 scenes from MGM musicals.

LUCKY LADY (US 1975)
Prod/Michael Gruskoff. Dir/Stanley Donen. Scr/Willard Huyck, Gloria Katz. Music/Ralph Burns. Ph/Geoffrey Unsworth. Colour by DeLuxe. GB distribution/20th

This page: working for the first time with her father on A Matter of Time

Opposite: in New York, New York

Century-Fox. Certificate AA. 118 mins.
With: (Gene Hackman (Kibby), Liza Minnelli (Claire), Burt Reynolds (Walker), Geoffrey Lewis (Captain Aaron Mosely), John Hillerman (Christy McTeague), Robby Benson (Billy Weber), Michael Horden (Captain Rockwell)
Minnelli, Hackman and Reynolds star as three amateur rum-runners in 1930s America, who have an entangled relationship with the law in the daytime and with each other outside of business hours.

A MATTER OF TIME (US/Italy 1976)

Prod/Jack H Skirball, J Edmund Grainger. Scr/Vincente Minnelli. Scr/John Gay, based on a novel by Maurice Druon. Music/George Gershwin, John Kander, Fred Ebb. Ph/ Geoffrey Unsworth. 99 mins.
With: Liza Minnelli, Ingrid Bergman, Charles Boyer
Finally teamed with her director father, Liza plays the part of an Italian villager working as a chambermaid in pre-World War I Rome. There she is taught sophistication through the stories of an eccentric old Contessa (Ingrid Bergman), whose past the maid imagines with herself being in the position of the Contessa. The film must have been a disappointment for both

Minnelli senior and junior as it was savagely edited before being released and received equally savage notices from the critics.

SILENT MOVIE (US 1976)

Prod/Michael Hertzberg. Dir/Mel Brooks. Scr/Mel Brooks, Ron Clark, Rudy De Luca, Barry Levinson. Music/John Morris. Ph/Paul Lohmann. Colour by DeLuxe. GB distribution/20th Century-Fox. Certificate A. 87 mins.
With: Mel Brookes (Mel Funn), Marty Feldman (Mart Eggs), Dom DeLuise (Dom Bell), Bernadette Peters (Vilma Kaplan), Sid Caesar (Studio Chief), Harold Gould (Engulf), Ron Carey (Devour), Carol Arthur (Pregnant Lady), Liam Dunn (Newsvendor), Burt Reynolds, James Caan, Liza Minnelli, Anne Bancroft, Marcel Marceau, Paul Newman (themselves).
Mel Brooks chose silent films as the target for another in his series of spoofs, following *Blazing Saddles* and *Young Frankenstein*. The plot followed silent movie producer Mel Funn (Brooks) trying to gather a group of superstars to make a new 1920s feature to save an ailing studio. Rather than have actors portray 1920s stars, he persuaded various modern-day

NEW YORK

stars to spoof themselves. Along with Liza Minnelli were Burt Reynolds, James Caan, Anne Bancroft, Marcel Marceau and Paul Newman.

NEW YORK, NEW YORK (US 1977)

Prod/Irwin Winkler. Dir/Martin Scorsese. Scr/Earl Mac Rauch, Mardik Martin. Music/Ralph Burns. Ph/Laszlo Kovacs. Technicolor. GB distribution/United Artists. Certificate A. 153 mins.

With: Liza Minnelli (Francine Evans), Robert DeNiro (Jimmy Doyle), Lionel Stander (Tony Harwell), Barry Primus (Paul Wilson), Mary Kay Place (Bernice), Georgie Auld (Frankie Harte)

A total departure to the traditional Hollywood musical with which her mother was so accustomed, *New York, New York* presented the grimmer side of the touring big bands of the 1940s. Robert DeNiro starred as a repulsive bandleader, who became lover and husband to his leading singer, played by Liza Minnelli. Despite Martin Scorsese's direction and excellent character parts by Minnelli and DeNiro, many believed this film to suffer by being too long (20 minutes have been cut since the original release print).

This page: with Albert Finney in Charlie Bubbles

Opposite: in New York, New York

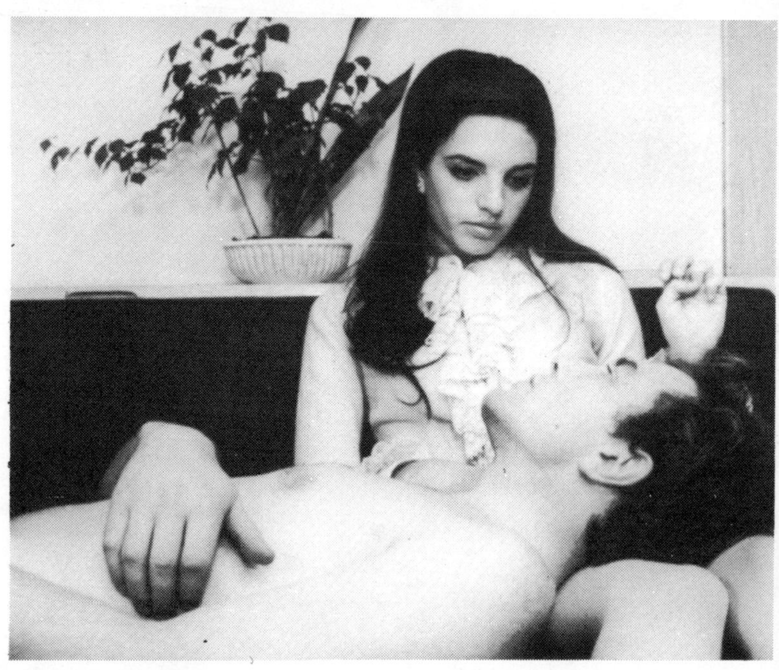

ARTHUR (US 1981)

Prod/Robert Greenhut. Dir-scr/Steve Gordon. Music/Burt Bacharach. Ph/Fred Schuler. Technicolor. GB distribution/ Columbia-EMI-Warner (Warner). Certificate AA. 97 mins. With: Dudley Moore (Arthur Bach), Liza Minnelli (Linda Marolla), John Gielgud (Hobson), Geraldine Fitzgerald (Martha Bach), Jill Eikenberry (Susan Johnson), Stephen Elliott (Burt Johnson)

Caught up in the wave of fame and recognition for so long denied him until *10*, Dudley Moore rose to giddier heights when co-starring with Liza Minnelli in *Arthur*. Much of Liza's appeal comes across in the character of Linda Marolla, an aspiring student actress for whom Arthur (Dudley Moore) risks losing his £400 million inheritance. Arthur's family are intent on him marrying the "right" girl, Susan Johnson the perfectly charming and pretty daughter of a top gangster turned businessman. Arthur, a spoilt and invariably drunken playboy, develops other ideas soon after meeting Linda Marolla. The whacky Arthur risks inheritance and even his life to hold on to the offbeat Linda in this box office record breaker which proved to be an excellent choice of film for Liza Minnelli to make her long-overdue return to the screen.

This page: with John Gielgud in   Arthur

Opposite: a publicity shot for CBS

Overleaf: two scenes from Arthur   with Dudley Moore